INTRODUCTION TO CLOUD CARE

Laura Theis writes in her second language. Her Elgin-Award-nominated debut *how to extricate yourself*, an Oxford Poetry Library Book-of-the-Month, won the Brian Dempsey Memorial Prize. *A Spotter's Guide To Invisible Things* received the Live Canon Collection Prize and the Society of Authors' Arthur-Welton-Award. Other accolades include the Alpine Fellowship Writing Prize, Poets&Players Prize, Oxford Brookes Poetry Prize, AM Heath Prize, and Mogford Prize. Her children's debut *Poems from a Witch's Pocket* (Emma Press) will be published in autumn 2025.

Also by Laura Theis

A Spotter's Guide To Invisible Things   (Live Canon, 2023)

how to extricate yourself   (Dempsey & Windle, 2020)

PRAISE for *Introduction to Cloud Care*

Introduction to Cloud Care struck me with its tenderness and warmth: reading it felt like a springtime walk or seeing your kindest friend at a party. Through a range of encounters and transformations—with an unborn daughter, a dandelion-therapist, the haunting characters of Hansel and Gretel—beauty 'is never a question'. Simultaneously, these poems are not naive, bearing witness to trees awaiting 'their respective beheadings', and deeply in touch with their instincts, ready to 'run / as soon as running's required.' Read it in a meadow, under an oak tree, or hidden in the shed at a house party."

— Bryony Littlefair

In Laura Theis' third collection, published by the inimitable Broken Sleep Books, clouds wait to be asked the right question, muntjac apparitions emerge out of nowhere, daffodils bloom from under sofas and a non-existent child chides her mother for lack of empathy. Surreal, blissful and mesmerising, with each poem effortlessly revealing fresh amazements of the kind we experienced as children turning the pages of our first stories, *Introduction to Cloud Care* already has the hallmark of a classic — coming as it does from a mind infused by fairy tales and 'dark forests/ grimm siblings'. I loved spending time in Laura's magical world and plan to revisit often.

— Jenny Lewis

Inside the light and air of Laura Theis's poems, you will find beautiful and sensitive stories of our connection to the natural world and wry observations of desire and the human search for intimacy. This is touching, funny, truly gorgeous writing.

— Vanessa Lampert

ISBN: 978-1-916938-77-9

Cover designed by Aaron Kent

Edited by Charley Barnes

Typeset by Aaron Kent

Broken Sleep Books Ltd
PO BOX 102
Llandysul
SA44 9BG

CONTENTS

for Ina M.
in memoriam

Introduction to Cloud Care

Laura Theis

Broken Sleep Books

INTRODUCTION TO CLOUD CARE

colours are floating
through the city
at tree height
in tired but festive clouds

pale oak green
liberal swathes of gold
some nuanced red
a little blue

the shadows they throw on the ground
form a uniform lacework of dark and dark
but you would have to stand
below them to see this

for most people watching
from the towers right above
this tenebrous commonality
stays a secret

but what of the clouds themselves?
do they know this
about each other?
these are of course the wrong questions

and you should not ask them
the clouds prefer this
they may seek you out
trail you home

when they float so low you could touch them
without lifting a hand (which they know you will not)
just let them rest a little near the timidity of your mind
until it's their time

MY SHRINK IS A DANDELION

which, first of all, means
that my therapy is free

which is handy because I have zero
money left to do anything

but lay face down
in a meadow and stare

at her edible leaves
while absorbing her words of wisdom.

'What you and I have in common,'
she says, *'is that there comes a time in our lives*

when we must break into stars
with our pleasure.'

I smile. She wears
her magic so lightly.

I want to ask her why she was named
for a lion's tooth when nothing about her is

frightening, when her face is a sun,
which is also a clock, which is also

a soft moon onto which I want to hang
my biggest wish.

Instead I say, *'How come you call yourself a shrink*
when you grow taller each time I see you?'

because my best therapy is making her shake a little,
suppressing a starburst of giggles.

POEM FROM A WITCH'S POCKET
for E. Willis

this is not how I remember it at all
my favourite line from your poem
that I carried with me for seven years
the one I chose to live by around
other people's rosemary bushes and cherry trees
the one I was even ready to steal
from you as a title for one of my own
I always thought you said *whenever a witch sees something she likes*
she will put it in her pocket
but listening to your reading I realise
it was a false memory all this time
your stanza talks instead about a witch
slipping the thing she desires into her glove
which is confusing to me
what kinds of gloves are we talking?
gardening gloves? what witch would need them?
or evening gloves? the long black velvet kind
that only movie stars wear? maybe flying gloves
for better grip on a broomstick?
and as for the thing that is not hers
where is the line between desire and fancy?
you will never know Willis
but I've taken this small thing
I wanted from you
made it mine
I like how it feels in my pocket
so dear against my ungloved hand

THE LISTENER

her magic was so gentle
you may not have known it
for a spell

the way she was able to listen so openly
that we were each coaxed into speaking
our language

the fiddle began to talk
of the willow tree it had been
how it had feasted on light and liquid

how it had swayed and creaked
in the wind like a door
to another realm

the piano confessed how its beauty was forged
from the killing of a playful giant who had loved
his life of mischief and joy

while the rain outside sang along in the dangerous language of water
a complicated grammar of clouds and droplets
stillness and rush

even the silence afterwards surprised itself
for the first time
in the mirror of her quiet attention

and bowed like a secret word
that had suddenly understood
its own significance

THREE IN TRANSLATION

the memory knocks and waits
for my welcome

> it's wearing a three-way
> grin and a battered hat

>> I hesitate before I dare
>> to let it enter because

old feelings aren't supposed to be reheated
like leftover takeaway

> I say *none of us are the same*
> *people we were back then*

>> *we each dream*
>> *in different languages now*

I wonder whether and how
that has changed things

> recalling our conversation
> before leaving for our separate countries

my mind overdubs our words
as a matter of course

translating between
old and new tongues

      as if it might render every regret
      a hazard of words that might still be said

A SMALL HAUNTING

every visit from me

a small haunting

and for hours, even days afterwards

a flourishing,

vanishing and flourishing

of inexplicable sadnesses

like fireflies

I have tried to be less moonlike

less translucent

but it doesn't seem to make much

of a difference

whether or not I am airborne

whether I am silent

whether I slip away leaving gifts

I TRY TO WRITE A LOVE POEM FOR SIGUNE SCHNABEL
BUT IT ONLY GOES MEDIUM WELL

I have trapped myself inside a library, at a desk by the large round
window. The winter branches below are hung with small brown

grenades, waving to draw my attention towards
the poet Sigune Schnabel scattering her eyes across the street.

What a strange thing it is to try and befriend a poet in another
language. We never seem to speak to each other;

rather angle for meaning and, if we catch a fractured word, lay the
sound back to earth.

Sometimes when we walk together the coltsfoot blooms at the edge
of our path and words fall soundlessly down the hours.

We stumble over wasteland and grass,
skin our questions.

A little time will pass, and we'll wonder: do our trajectories converge
like forgotten diamonds?

Then she tells me someone she knows is in bed with a bad case of prose.

She tells me all night strange animals have been coming into her
house. I say how I had a horse once

his name was Deadpan Prairie Martyr Observe Jackal Power Magic
Tomato Terrace. And she would say, *did I ever tell you*

about the country up north that hugs the senses like a sword, how it lies
in front of you, clouded with goose gray?

And if it were my wish, she'd describe the gull-white storied walls
of clouds, how the winds tear from the west waves on the high dike.

And then she would ask me what I like, especially in the morning:
when the light comes again like love

all the signals of the past reminding us how we slang we sunk
and sung in gravel how the brisk rain capsized us

made us each other's damp companions through a coldening universe,

the city observing us, as if it meant to say: now I will require your
help, propose!

And I would say, Ms Schnabel, Sigune, I am vitreous! And when my
chest heaves (I cannot prevent it) the transparent walls are

wetted with salt drops and damn near cracking! So much for a, yes,
glass heart wishing it was sand again

and Sigune, Sigune listen I will let you talk
of sea spark or leaf song or the crane dance on the tideway,

but I will confess also the tricks of my heart, so hard and
translucent, I won't hide it from you.

THERE USED TO BE A HOUSE HERE

but now it's a tree-walled
ruin under an open sky

she has learned that
the generosity of birds is

a witchcraft beyond
pendulums or sage

the magpies come on thursdays
to share their surprising bounty

from coins to
engagement rings

other birds bring blades
or a gift of feathers

to stuff into quilts
keep the night frosts at bay

she knows them by song
she hopes for a key

back into the shelter
of sleep

the one magic that still holds
power

THE MUSIC OF DUST

once you've been here
as long as we have

you too will learn to listen
out for the dry music of dust

as you inch along our
grief-struck lanes

it will orbit you
like a memory

and like a faithful homing pigeon
its message will always find you

to sing of the things
it must cover

(there's nothing
it can't cover up)

to sing of its own rise and fall
and how there is never

a single second
it ceases to dance

A LESSON IN ROSEWOOD

today we are sad
my non-existent daughter
says and squeezes my dry hand
with her sticky one

I nod and smile but
she shakes her perfect
non-existent head of curls
tells me to smile more sadly

when I oblige
with a quivering lip
a quiet stream of tears
she still isn't satisfied

no no like this
look at me
you have to wail
because you mean it

she tells me sadness is meant to be
audible to those around you
that it should be
a summons

she has always been my best teacher
she has been smarter than me
since she was a zygote
who refused to enter this world

as a girl
with briar in her chest

OAK COPPICE

Just yesterday the world burnt.
Today I'm sitting beneath the upturned
roots of a great oak, where the blue-dotted sheep's wool
hangs in garlands like Spanish moss.

Everything seems at peace. Verdant and ancient. Time is slowed
to something less painful
by the grey rocks and cicadas,
the breeze.

Poets have told me over and over about sitting in nature,
staying away from screens. But I am typing this on my phone.
I wish I had not looked up
the meaning of coppice.

The trees behind me
rustle and sway
as they patiently wait for
their respective beheadings.

GIFTED

we don't know how many witches exactly
we asked to her christening

and how many others appeared
uninvited and offended at the slight

witches are hard to count and their gifts
may be hard to account for

we are still trying to puzzle out which ones
were meant as curses and which ones

will turn out to be favours
we've kept them all to be safe

put some in storage in a shoe box under her bed
next to her collection of interesting pebbles

sometimes she lays them all out
takes one and holds it in her palm like a small sun

to examine it closely
here is my wildness she might say

my inconsistency
my flair for maniacal dance moves

my brittle temper and look here are all
the echoes of you that sorrow inside me

and demand to be turned
into song

KINDRED

I think I would know you
by your voice first.

It is not important
when or where we would meet.

Maybe you'd be armed
with a sharing

bowl of cherries,
a pot of cinnamon tea,

a small dark bird on your shoulder.
But this is how I would understand you:

the moment you start reading
aloud, become a different person

lost
to any other world

but this imaginary one. There'd be a
point where you'd look up at me,

recognising me by my joy at just
sitting there listening to you

until the story is complete.
How ready you are

for my silence and the library
of songs in my head. Already an eager

scholar of my strangest dreams.
Unsurprised when I turn

into a bird just like yours,
but delighted to watch us fly.

SOME POINTERS ON DATING A WERE-HARE

you may be starting to notice
certain traits about me:

the unnatural speed
of my heartbeat

the eerie gold of my eyes
opaque with mistrust

my love of tender shoots
and root vegetables

how I can't seem to help
chewing pencils to shreds

the way I keep my distance
from dogs of all sizes and never

text you back on nights
when the full moon is out

there is no known cure so
I never wonder how long

we'll be able to go on
all I think is how fast I will run

as soon as running's required
you might say I won't need to

but I'm easily startled
and bolting's how I survive

GOOD PARTY

if you cried today
you are invited

if you have been talking
to no one
but trees
you are invited

if your best friend
is a ghost
on a string
you are invited

if you have nothing
to wear
but a threadbare
smile you are invited

if you came secretly clutching
a book
just in case
you are invited

if people's faces and names
blow through you
like air
you are invited

if you know you'll sneak out
ten minutes in
without saying goodbye
you are invited

I promise
you
are
invited

I will do
whatever I can
to make this
your kind of party

THE BEES

I'm looking forward to
meeting the bees

you say the noise that they make
in their winter sleep is a mix of the hiss

of an ocean wave
and the hush of a secret to keep

shhhhhhhh

I'm looking forward to
hearing that sound

my ears are thrilled that we're allowed
to snatch snippets

from this world of the small
and the many

shhhhhhhh

I'm looking forward
to singing for bees

I am told that they dance
so magnificently

we don't share a language but we do
share a love for things that cannot really be

put into words

OBITUARY IN SIX LINES

the poem was a machine
for becoming more feral

it wanted to reverse time
unmelt our glaciers

scab the woulds we inflicted
with sempiternal moss

NARCISSISTIC NATURE POEM

riverbeds, oceans, look at me now
I'm trying to talk to you

stay the night
praise and reassure me - don't criticise -

tell me I'm more ravishing today
than I will be tomorrow

adore me as I adore nothing
but the night

tell me you will never tire of my
tempers and my selfishness

tell me you see me
and that I'm forgiven

oh and earth what can I say
you may have heard yourself described

just as I was today: 'on fire'
yes we are both smoking

hot in different ways
is this not a good thing?

I've never met anybody my love
did not incinerate

AN ENTRY FROM THE SPOTTER'S GUIDE FOR INVISIBLE THINGS

this coast line
marks the quiet
border between your old

life and every invaluable
breath you will decide
to take in this one

an invisible moon is
pulling invisible
tricks on the water

slighting the sand
forts against
a raspberry sky

I WONDER HOW OVID DEALT WITH THIS

I'm writing a book about transformations, but as you can imagine I'm having a world of trouble with it. Sometimes it shapeshifts in the middle of a sentence, growing wings or legs and I have to run after it for hours. Sometimes overnight it transforms into a steaming bowl of soup and tries to trick me into eating it for breakfast. Sometimes there's no bowl, just a patch of wet on my desk that goes from vapour to ice to red wine. When I have people coming round they point at it, saying things like *I love your new sofa* or *I had no idea you keep miniature leopards*. I sigh and insist that it is in fact my work in progress, and they nod and smile, then make up excuses to leave. My editor calls to thank me for the surprise bonsai I sent, but when can she have my manuscript please? I try to explain. She understands when it morphs into a giant balloon before her very eyes and she tells me it will need more work. I cry a bit on the phone, saying *how will I know when it's ready? How will I recognise its final shape? Maybe,* she says very gently, w*hen it starts transforming itself more willingly into something resembling a book?* So here I am at it again, trying a different approach. I've given up writing. When the book turns into a lamp, I dress up as Aladdin. When it's a mat, I start doing yoga. When it's a fish, I play with it in the bathtub. When it's a horse, I go riding out on an adventure. When it's an elaborate dress, I go to a ball. I don't know if there's going to be anything much to show for it by the end, but I can already tell my life is being transformed...

FERAL TALE

the most beautiful sight
I have ever seen is
the rage of one woman
avalanching into
the rage of ten
thousand more

I want to be saved
by the fury of women
I want to dangle my long woven hair
from the towering rage of women
I want the whole hog
golden carriage and steed

I want to wear my most elaborate
dress to the dance
with the bravery of women
and when I lose any glass
slippery part of myself I want to lose it
to the sisterhood of women

I want the whole world to
watch as I marry
the fury of women
and when death do
us part I want my bones
to lie alongside the ferocious
beauty of women

unbroken ever after

RIVALS

My lover returns from her walks
happy and smelling unmistakably
of sex.

I know for a fact
that she is not meeting up with another
human soul, it's not that.

But I've seen the way she stares out
at the forest through
our bedroom window.

The way the wild cherries wave at her
like runaway brides, the way the birches
caress her with their overreaching branches.

I once watched her sling her arms around
an oak's trunk, unguarded
in a way she never will or would be with me.

I've seen the way she sighs and sinks into the peat moss,
her silence swept up in the flood of bird noise
which understands everything, asks for nothing.

She returns home to me with leaves in her hair,
her cheeks flushed,
always satisfied, serene.

Meanwhile I chop our firewood, stoke the log
burner and understand, as the smoke gets in my eyes,
that she will never truly be mine.

STĀN (A PAUL MULDOON GOLDEN SHOVEL)

he was a
small brown rock
and I was his accidental god
carrying him toward the waiting
palm of his future in
my coat pocket: a mode of travel that the
hitherto stationary rock experienced as akin to having wings

when I tried to
part ways he confessed he never wanted to be set
down again, never be as helpless to move by himself
as I'd found him in the spot he'd waited before
and by obliging the
rock's wish I've now turned myself into a river, his lapidary, his king

SEA-SMOOTHED STONE

many believe that translating death
into words is a poet's work
but language folds at the edges of life

so now I find I cannot speak
of what I forced myself
to witness

no try-hard magician can summon
a bunch of flowers
out of a black hole

even if I named only the rosemary
needles crumbling to dust
in my pocket

the strange forbearance
of the sea-smoothed stone
in my fist

the fraudulent light
of the plastic candle
on the hospital nightstand

I could not face it
I could not bear it
what use are poems if I still cannot bear it

BEAUTY

she likes to sneak up on the bridge-bound suicide
saying *all this river for you to look at*

she's confusing
our hearts for leaves

keep living
she's never a question

she's the singing trees
she's an amber dog's grief

she's the reason we think we need
flowers at funerals

A PART OF ME IS STILL SECRETLY HOPING YOU
FAKED IT

When I heard about what had happened
I went back to the book we had all been published in
and there was your bio:
Born in France and has not died yet.
Like a punch to the stomach.

You were the kind of person that once met
would be remembered forever.
Larger than life, perhaps
too large for life to contain you.
We were never friends.

In fact, I believe you quite disliked me.
But you let me see glimpses of sweetness
poking out from behind the pretentious public persona,
a half-bored half-contemptuous intellectual superior
with a heart for squashing, just like the rest of us.

Rose told me you were secretly kind to her,
called her little healer in your exaggerated accent.
I remember what you made us all play the first night we met.
A game for poets, of mismatched questions and answers.
What is a tooth? A box that must not be unlocked.

The last time we talked I was lying in a hammock,
rattling down the names of people
whose existence had already been wiped from your mind.

You, who made it your mission to be so utterly
unforgettable.

It seems there is a kind of mourning village
spreading across countries with the news.
If no one had told us, I might have imagined you out
in the world still, in a striped T-shirt or a ridiculous suit,
a rollie in your hand, taking anachronistically analogue pictures

of astounding beauty or playing your Oud in Morocco.
Or back in Oxford getting drunk while pretending to work
in that little whiskey shop. You were named for a stone.
You were so unafraid of being a cliché you
could not flinch to save your life.

SITO

how could I ever bring myself to say
that it may never happen

how could I tell you about bread and fear
a feast of solitude

how could I ever prepare you to tell
the women from the pain

when you ask me what weighs heavier
the feather or the fog

when you ask to sing of what spring might be
the dream of the flower loaf

forgive me not only for the silence but also
for what this silence suggests

the distance is an audible frost
one note held which once lost

turns to silver
I promise

I cannot teach you more than this winter desert
the cold sands hold the same knowledge with more eloquence

ΑΓΡΥΠΝΙΑ / AGRYPNIA

the night has shrunk

to a silver sliver

spilling over

into morning

specks of light

dappling questions

on your lover's

secretive hair

A LUNAR RENAMING

I am burning last year's
lilac and planting new ranunculus

the quiet murmur of
gossiping grapevines

informs me the flower moon has renamed herself
the moon of letting go

a name that seems like it should only belong
to autumn's falling leaves

but the truth is
the closer we get to winter

the more tightly we hold on
guarding ourselves like nuclear codes

whereas may is
for cleaning dark corners

allowing the soul
to shift again

the most open-handed month
when nothing is ordinary

when blossom appears overnight
only to snow down

cover the world in farewell
white

A PORTRAIT

Do you know that kind of joy which returns
to your fingernails with a crackle?

The budding daffodils
peeking out from under the sofa?

The first smell of spring
right there next to your bed?

Or maybe if you imagine the far-away whinny
of a shire horse from the inside of your pocket?

Or, in the dark of the ocean,
the gleam of a single incisor?

A big toe spray-dancing and then
returning serenely to shore?

Or no, maybe this one comes closest: a lost eyelash
lying very still beneath a corkscrew birch in the park.

She is precisely like that.

SELF-CARE FÜR UNSICHTBARE

ok so if it gets bad you must
cover yourself in old mown grass
trace the lines of your face
with a horsetail stalk
stick your bare feet
into an unknown river
step on something sharp then
pull the thorn out of your own toe
even though the angle is awkward
put a little plaster on it and say
there - good as new

CRUMBS DIPTYCH

I.

You were so young the first time your parents tried to murder you.
Putting your trust in breadcrumbs
when you should have put your trust
in the birds.

And the crazy old lady with her edible house -
wasn't she justifiably upset when you started
munching her walls?
She was always worried about that place.

Especially her sugar-spun roof
when it inevitably rained in that forest.
But she still took you in.
She still fed you.

She was still as good a mother as she could be to her foundlings.
However you had been raised in the language of cruelty.
You burnt and ate her
without a grain of remorse.

And afterwards, you burnt it all down, the entire forest.
The flames spread as far as the woodcutter's hut.
They say you laughed at the ashes.
You swore you'd never go hungry again.

II.

once upon a time
I was all of these:

the desperate father and also
the children he leads away from the safety of home
into the deep forest dark
so a story can happen

and also the witch that waits
with the treats
on the other end
grinning

I was also those crumbs that happen
to get consumed
before they can fulfil
their intended purpose

I was the oblivious birds that don't give
two shits about the other storyline
assuming the unexpected feast was always
meant for no one else to find

I was the hut that's
too small for four hungry people
and the big house that would willingly
let itself be eaten

I was also the cage and the stick and the fire
the homicidal girl yes I even was happily ever after: once
for a time

A FLYING VISIT TO THE WRITER'S ZOO

and here we have
the poets:

they are nocturnal creatures
who dwell in liminal spaces

shy little monsters
subsisting on a mixed diet

of intrusive thoughts
echoes of past loves

and occasionally
beans on toast

approach at your own risk
they might try to escape

using your head
as their getaway driver

FIRST NIGHT

I count the stars from
under the skylight: ten without
moving my head. Did the people

who slept here before me
give a name to this constellation?
The house won't say. We'll have to

be patient with each other, both grieving
our exes. But it's a good sign that it made me
stub my toe on its stairs when it caught me

thinking about the old home too much.
I got the message, scrubbed its floors as well
as I could. The house forgave me with sunset,

birdsong on its roof
and the soft drums of October
against the panes.

THE BEST YEARS ARE THE ONES YOU CREATE SPACE

you ask me what of the past
year I want to burn

and my first thought is
the songlessness

I want to be part of a chanting
crowd again

I want unheard-of melody
and harmonies

to find all the buried music
inside of me and pass it around

to strangers

TRANSFORMATION DAY

Today I take my true shape.
Growing, thirsting, swallowing everything.
A guzzling, swirling lemonade of debris,
I'm breaking the bank, breaking all the banks.
I'm coming up taller than the cows.
I make new real estate to please the up-and-coming
gulls. I hightail it into several cellars, pubs and living
rooms, redirect the traffic and atomise a million people's
travel plans. Everyone will need to make a special effort
to cross me and do it gingerly, in a funny tiptoeing way
but no matter how carefully they tread
I'll still fill their boots to the brim
with wet, and they'll just have to suck
it up, continue on their way squelching.
I've always preferred to live as if someone else would
have to come sort out the mess.

A LAZY CLAIRVOYANT PREDICTS HER OWN FUTURE
WITH HER PHONE'S AUTOCOMPLETE

my future is going well thanks
I really hope I haven't made you
disappear

my future is going to be
full of summer moments I didn't get
around to

my future is going to be treated
as the winner
when we touch the wolf

I have a poem in which I use the words wolf
it down into our satchels and pretend
it isn't there

I have a summer
I have a poem
I think you should meet

I have a poem in which I use the words
I have a future
I already know

my future is more than a distant relative
my future is moon between us
and the orb

tonight the clairvoyant is missing

a little detail

from the last two years

the other world is born

out of nothing

the poem is very enthusiastic about it all

TRUE STORY

It's early morning, and there's a little muntjac in our garden. Mesmerised, the dog and I both stare as he chews on frosted leaves, old windfall apples. The garden is by necessity one hundred percent escape proof, surrounded by unjumpable fences on all sides. *So how on earth?* The muntjac raises a halfmoon-crowned poker face towards us, and smugly, practically winking, turns himself invisible again. The dog and I look at each other like, *what the actual fuck, have we both lost our marbles?* We go out to investigate the apparition's vanishing. There is a single hoofprint in the mud, but although we sniff around until the clouds conceal the daytime moon, we find no magic portal to a fairy realm, nor any more mundane explanation of the trick... *It's almost comforting,* I tell the dog as we go back inside, *to be reminded we are not the boss of anything.*

A BODY MAP

name it the kindness of water
the part of you that knows when to be quiet
or how to let go

and the part that knows
when to lay your head heavy on somebody's knee
name it the kindness of bones

we are born into it as our first language
the kindness of air, of skin and nails, tongues
the kindness of teeth

but the dumbest, bravest part of you
the sad lucky lump that keeps on beating
the odds: name it heart

IMAGINE A FIELD

imagine a field
disturbed by nobody

imagine the firs
that grow beyond it

and the furry spirits
they shelter

imagine late hawthorn rubies on
bare-spined branches

dirt puddles
frozen into abstract paintings

imagine yourself walking
into this scene

and lying down
on the cold ground

imagine what colour
the sky would be

and how many
sharp-winged birds

you'd witness
crossing above you

imagine closing your eyes
and your retinas painting

an afterimage
of avian patterns

you've made such a habit
of seeing yourself as a prisoner

but look at this picture of you
surrounded by free things

how you fit right in

VOLARY

I have known for a while now
that I am in control of the birds

yes you have me to thank for the
dawn chorus delay

but don't thank me yet
I am also responsible

for the black and white streaks
of pigeon poop on your window

and the time that massive one landed
right on your head on the way home from the salon

I also made them devour your cherry harvest
before you could pick a single red jewel for yourself

but don't hate me yet
because I make the blackbirds

and thrushes sing
you to sleep I make the ducks

form a little regatta on the river
as you cycle past towards work

I always send you magpies
in pairs but starlings in clouds and

the best shrieking
kites to make you look up

from your phone and take in
the maddening scope of the sky

every feather you find
is a message from me

and if the singing goes quiet you'll know
what it means

TRUTH BOMB

listen I grew up
in a suburb

where each street was named
for a fairy tale

in the land of dark forests
grimm siblings

and in my mother tongue
which brought you

rapunzel and rumpelstiltskin
no story ends

in a twee happily
ever after

it's all much more conditional and ominous
our endings don't mention happiness

instead our folk tales sign off this way:
and if they managed not to die

they're still knocking about
somewhere to this day

ACKNOWLEDGEMENTS

Thank you to my wonderful publishers Broken Sleep Books - Aaron for making it all possible and Charley for your editing expertise and gentle encouragement...

Léonie, Sophie, Jennie, Jess, (and of course Rosie and Eva and Baby Gus) I know I would never ever get any writing done if it weren't for our Friday nights and I'm so incredibly excited for all your amazing projects and books...

Clare, Jak, Harriet & Cesca, thank you for all your beautiful brilliant words and for being the best and most supportive Storytellers Supper Club in the world...

Phoebe, Rowena, Jak & Maya, thank you for all the cosy and delicious Poetry & Pancakes...

Everyone at LIT and OPL and Catweazle, Lucy, Kiran, Tom, Jess, Sarvat, Daisy, Matt, Pia, Steffi, Klaus, Fab, Helen, Hannah, James, Calum, Sam, Ditte, Anders, Claire, Aget, Ella, Vicky, Chris, Sam, Rose, and MK, all the wonderful editors, teachers, workshop leaders and the whole poetry community, and most especially you wonderful people who are reading this book, I am so grateful...

My lovely family, for making so much space on your bookshelves and always being my very best customers...

Sam, I wrote all these when Kara was still alive and I know I will never forget her....

Nick, I know thank you doesn't even begin to touch the sides but...thank you my love.

With thanks to these places for the first publication of these poems:

a lazy clairvoyant predicts her own future with her phone's autocomplete - with gratitude to *Wet Grain*

A Flying Visit To The Writer's Zoo - with gratitude to *Amsterdam Quarterly*

Three in Translation - with gratitude to *Vole Books*

Poem From A Witch's Pocket - with gratitude to *Postcards from the Archive*, Heidi Williamson, Sylee Gore and Elizabeth Willis

My shrink is a dandelion - with gratitude to *Candlestick Press*

I Try To Write A Love Poem For Sigune Schnabel But It Only Goes Medium Well - with gratitude to *Oxford Poetry* and Luke Allan

a lesson in rosewood - with gratitude to Glyn Maxwell and the *AUB Prize Anthology*

the bees - with gratitude to *The Caterpillar,* Mucho, Steffi, & Klaus

Feral Tale - with gratitude to the *Sisterhood Anthology*

an entry from the spotter's guide for invisible things - with gratitude to *Wildfire Words*

beauty - with gratitude to *frozen wavelets*

Rivals - with gratitude to *Berlin Lit*

Crumbs Diptych - with gratitude to *Makarelle*

First Night - with gratitude to *Welter*

the best years are the ones you create space - with gratitude to *Alchemy Spoon*

ἀγρυπνία / agrypnia - with gratitude to *harana*

sea-smoothed stone - with gratitude to the *Chesham Literature Festival*

Gifted, imagine a field, self-care für unsichtbare - with gratitude to *Ó'Bhéal*

Stān (A Paul Muldoon Golden Shovel) - with gratitude to *Spelt* and Paul Muldoon

truth bomb - with gratitude to *Ink, Sweat & Tears*

Sito - with gratitude to *Tinted Trails*

Some pointers on dating a were-hare - with gratitude to *Strange Horizons*

A Part Of Me Is Still Secretly Hoping You Faked It - with gratitude to the *Live Canon Anthology*

Kindred - with gratitude to *L'Audacia*

volary - with gratitude to *Passengers*

POST CREDITS EASTER EGG*
a frankenstein-poem stitched together from all the other poems' first lines in order of appearance in the book

colours are floating / which, first of all, means / this is not how I remember it at all

her magic was so gentle / the memory knocks and waits / every visit from me / I have trapped myself inside a library / but now it's a tree-walled ruin / you've been here *today*

we are sad / just yesterday the world burnt / we don't know how many witches exactly

I think I would know you / you may be starting to notice / I'm looking forward to / riverbeds, oceans, look at me now / this coast line / I'm writing

a book about transformations / my lover returns from her walks / many believe that translating death / she likes to sneak up

when I heard about what had happened / how could I ever bring myself to say / the night has shrunk / I am burning last

do you know that kind of joy which returns / ok so if it gets bad you must / you were so young the first time your parents tried to murder you / I count the stars / today I take

my true shape / my future is going well thanks / name it the kindness of water / imagine

a field / it's early morning / I have known for a while now

listen I grew up

LAY OUT YOUR UNREST